Sports Illustrated KIDS

BASEBALL'S GREATEST

WALK-OFFS

AND OTHER CRUNCH-TIME HEROICS

BY MATT CHANDLER

T0052471

CAPSTONE PRESS
a capstone imprint

Captivate is published by Capstone Press, an imprint of Capstone.
1710 Roe Crest Drive, North Mankato, Minnesota 56003
www.capstonepub.com

Library of Congress Cataloging-in-Publication Data is available on the Library of Congress website.
ISBN 978-1-4966-8730-2 (library binding)
ISBN 978-1-4966-8736-4 (paperback)
ISBN 978-1-4966-8737-1 (ebook PDF)

Summary: When the stakes are high, some players seize the moment and make themselves legends. From pitching heroics in Game 7 of the World Series to pennant-clinching home runs, some of baseball's greatest moments are chronicled in vivid fashion here. You've got a front-row seat to the action.

Editorial Credits
Bobbie Nuytten, designer; Eric Gohl, media researcher; Katy LaVigne, production specialist

Photo Credits
AP Photo: Fred Jewell, 9; Getty Images: Bettmann, 35, Bob Levey, 7, Boston Red Sox/Billie Weiss, 17, Ezra Shaw, 27, Jonathan Daniel, 25, Photo File, 37, Stringer/Jason Miller, 33, Stringer/Stacy Revere, 19, Tom Szczerbowski, 11; Newscom: Reuters/Mike Segar, 5, Reuters/Ray Stubblebine, 21, UPI/Ronald Martinez, 30, USA Today Sports/Robert Hanashiro, 41; Shutterstock: Beto Chagas, cover (stadium), 1, Eugene Onischenko, cover (player), silvae, cover (lights), 1, Vasyl Shulga, cover (field), 1; Sports Illustrated: Al Tielemans, 23, Chuck Solomon, 29, Heinz Kluetmeier, 43, John Biever, 13, V.J. Lovero, 15

Printed and bound in the USA.
PA117

TABLE OF CONTENTS

Words in **bold** are in the glossary.

GAME-ENDING GREATNESS

Baseball is a game of **strategy**. Pinch hitters, intentional walks, **suicide squeezes**, and stolen bases are important parts of the game.

For all of its strategy, baseball is still a game of individual moments. One pitch can instantly change the outcome of a game. One defensive play can steal a victory from the other team.

Often, those big moments come at the end of a game. A two-out, two-strike home run. A strikeout with the bases loaded. A center fielder climbing the wall to grab a home run and pull it back into the park for the final out.

The **walk-off** win is one of the most dramatic moments in sports. Do you have a favorite walk-off moment from Major League Baseball (MLB)? If you don't yet, you might by the end of this book.

David Ortiz's walk-off home runs made him a legend in Boston. He led the Red Sox to a World Series win that ended the team's long, long championship drought.

CHAPTER ONE

HOME RUN HEROES

HOME RUN IN HOUSTON

It was Game 6 of the 2019 American League Championship Series. The hometown Houston Astros were locked in a 4–4 tie with the New York Yankees.

With two outs in the bottom of the ninth, the game looked like it was headed to extra innings. Then, Astros outfielder George Springer drew a walk from Yankees **closer** Aroldis Chapman. The Astros had a chance. Six-time All-Star second baseman José Altuve slowly walked to the plate.

Chapman fell behind 2–1 in the count. He needed to throw a strike. He left the fourth pitch in the at-bat high in the strike zone. Altuve turned on it and connected. There was no doubt the instant it left the bat. Altuve had just hit his 13th career postseason home run. He circled the bases and jogged into the waiting mob of teammates at home plate. The Astros were going to the World Series!

PLAYERS WITH THE MOST WALK-OFF HOME RUNS

Jim Thome, 13	Albert Pujols, 12
Jimmie Foxx, 12	Frank Robinson, 12
Mickey Mantle, 12	Babe Ruth, 12
Stan Musial, 12	

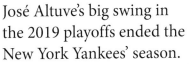

José Altuve's big swing in the 2019 playoffs ended the New York Yankees' season.

MARATHON GAME

The 14,754 fans who arrived at Comiskey Park in Chicago on May 8, 1984, were in for a long night. In fact, it was the beginning of a record-breaker. The White Sox were hosting the Milwaukee Brewers.

In the bottom of the ninth, Milwaukee led 4–2. The White Sox rallied for two runs to force extra innings.

The teams played another eight innings without scoring a run. After 17 innings, the umpires stopped play. It was 1 a.m. The teams returned the next day. They played almost a third full game before White Sox outfielder Harold Baines stepped to the plate in the bottom of the 25th inning. Baines turned on a fastball and drove it to dead center field.

Brewers center fielder Rick Manning leaped high in the air. The ball carried over his glove and over the wall. The White Sox won the game 7–6. At eight hours and six minutes long, it set the record for the longest Major League game in history.

Harold Baines ended a record-breaking game with a blast over the fence in center field. Baines was inducted into the Hall of Fame in 2019.

The longest game in minor league baseball also ended on a walk-off hit. The Pawtucket Red Sox beat the Rochester Red Wings in 33 innings. The 1981 game ended on a bases-loaded walk-off single by Dave Koza.

DOUBLE SLAM

Players like Ozzie Smith have made it into the National Baseball Hall of Fame without ever hitting a single grand slam. Then there are players like Toronto Blue Jays left fielder Steve Pearce. In 2017, Pearce hit two in the same week. Both of Pearce's slams were game-winning walk-offs.

Pearce hit the first slam while the Jays were locked in a 4–4 tie with the Oakland A's. Pearce came to the plate with the bases loaded and two outs in the bottom of the 10th inning. Pearce took a pitch from reliever Liam Hendriks and drove it to left field. The ball was hooking foul, but it landed in the seats just inside the foul pole for the walk-off grand slam.

Three days later the Jays trailed the Angels 10–7. Pearce delivered again. Angels reliever Bud Norris left a fastball high in the strike zone and Pearce jumped on it. He hit a towering home run to left field to give his Blue Jays their second walk-off win in three days.

Steve Pearce was the third player in Major League Baseball history to hit two walk-off grand slams in the same season. Cy Williams did it for the Phillies in 1926, and 60 years later, Seattle's Jim Presley completed the double slam.

WALK-OFF CHAMP

When you hit 612 home runs in your career, some are bound to be walk-offs. Longtime Cleveland Indians slugger Jim Thome crushed a record 13 walk-off home runs during his 22-year career. Only 27 players in history have hit 500 or more home runs. Thome's 500th was, you guessed it, a walk-off. He crushed it in 2007 as a member of the Chicago White Sox to beat the Los Angeles Angels.

A RETURN TO BASEBALL

In the fall of 2001, the New York Yankees were preparing to return to the postseason. They held a big lead in the American League East over the Boston Red Sox. The defending World Series Champions were favored to return to the Series. Then tragedy struck.

The September 11 terrorist attacks left New Yorkers reeling. Suddenly, baseball didn't seem so important. Major League Baseball canceled all games for a week. The Yankees' push for the **pennant** would have to wait.

When baseball resumed in the Bronx on September 25, 2001, emotions were raw. The Yankees invited members of the New York City first responder units to attend the game. Both teams celebrated the heroes of September 11. The Yankees, led by their future captain, Derek Jeter, gave New Yorkers something to smile about as they won the division and returned to the World Series.

Derek Jeter and the Yankees advanced to the World Series several weeks after the tragic 9/11 attacks on New York City.

WELCOME TO NOVEMBER BASEBALL

Game 4 of the World Series was a big one for Yankees fans. They trailed the Arizona Diamondbacks 2–1 in the series. They needed the win at home. The Yankees trailed by two runs in the bottom of the ninth. They fought back and tied the game. The stage was set for Derek Jeter to be the hero. Jeter had a strong season in 2001. He'd hit .311 with 21 home runs. But he hadn't been playing well in the World Series. He was just 1 for 11 in the first three games. When his team needed him most, however, Jeter delivered.

The game that began on October 31 ended minutes into November 1. It was the first Major League game ever played in November. At 12:04 a.m., Jeter made history. He slapped a pitch off of Byung-Hyun Kim into the right field seats for the walk-off home run. It was the first home run ever hit in November.

Derek Jeter delivered 10 walk-off at-bats in his Hall of Fame career. He even had a rare walk-off with the bases loaded in a game in 1997.

Jeter's teammates mobbed him as he reached home plate after hitting a game-winning home run soon after midnight.

CHAPTER TWO

GAME-SAVING DEFENSE

GAME-SAVING GRAB

The Boston Red Sox were taking on the Houston Astros in the 2018 American League Championship Series.

Though the Red Sox were leading 8–6 in the bottom of the ninth, reliever Craig Kimbrel fell apart. He walked the bases loaded and set the table for Astros third baseman Alex Bregman to win the game.

Bregman got a great pitch to hit. He smacked a line drive to left. Outfielder Andrew Benintendi raced in. He had two choices: He could pull up and field the ball, or he could try for the diving catch. If he let the ball drop, the game would be tied. If he dove and the ball got by him, the Astros would win the game.

Benintendi never hesitated. He sprinted in and laid out in a full dive, picking the ball right before it hit the ground. The ball game was over—the Red Sox won!

The biggest game-ending defensive play in history was one that got away. Armando Galarraga was one out away from pitching a **perfect game**. Teammate Miguel Cabrera fielded the final out deep in the hole and threw to Galarraga, covering first, to complete the perfect game. Though the runner was clearly out, umpire Jim Joyce blew the call and the perfect game was lost.

Andrew Benintendi lifts his glove after making a diving catch with the game on the line.

HOME RUN THIEF

In a 162-game season, every game counts. Teams regularly miss the playoffs by a single game. The Milwaukee Brewers kicked off the 2019 season by stealing a win with a walk-off web gem.

The Brew Crew was home against the St. Louis Cardinals. The home team held a 5–4 lead with two outs in the ninth. Josh Hader was one out away from **saving** his team's first win of the season.

José Martínez stepped up to the plate. The Cardinals slugger hit 17 home runs in 2018. Could he start 2019 with a long ball? Martinez connected on a 1–0 pitch, driving it deep toward the wall. Center fielder Lorenzo Cain tracked the ball to the wall. He timed his leap perfectly and pulled the game-tying home run back over the fence for the final out!

Lorenzo Cain jumps for a ball that looks like a home run in the making.

TRIPLE (PLAY) THREAT

The Philadelphia Phillies were on the road to take on the New York Mets in 2009. The Mets were leading 9–7 in the bottom of the ninth inning. But things looked bad for Phillies second baseman Eric Bruntlett. He made back-to-back poor defensive plays, giving the Mets two base runners with no outs.

Mets outfielder Jeff Francoeur stepped to the plate. He represented the game-winning run. Bruntlett saved the day with a historic, walk-off defensive play.

With the Mets calling for a double steal, Francoeur lined a ball up the middle. Bruntlett ranged to his right. He grabbed the line drive and stepped on second base, doubling off Luis Castillo. Then he tagged out Daniel Murphy, who was attempting to steal second. The ball game was over! Bruntlett became only the second player in MLB history to complete an unassisted game-ending triple play.

Bruntlett's unassisted triple play is **legendary** in Philadelphia. Still, the Phillies released him at the end of the 2009 season. He never played a Major League game again.

Eric Bruntlett tagged Daniel Murphy for the third out.

NO-HITTER, NO PROBLEM

Roy Halladay played 11 years in the Major Leagues without reaching the postseason. He finally got his chance when his Philadelphia Phillies reached the playoffs in 2010. Halladay took the mound for Game 1 of the National League Divisional Round.

Halladay shut down the Cincinnati Reds at home all night long. He was helped by some great defense. The Reds put 19 balls in play. It took sharp defense to steal a few base hits from the visitors.

With two outs in the ninth, Brandon Phillips almost stopped history from being made. He chopped a ball out in front of the plate. Catcher Carlos Ruiz leaped out and grabbed the ball. Ruiz had to jump out and throw around the runner. He barely beat the speedy Phillips by a step. His walk-off defensive gem helped seal only the second no-hitter in postseason history.

Roy Halladay delivers a pitch in a playoff game against the Reds.

CHAPTER THREE

CLUTCH HITS

SQUEEZING OUT A WIN

Pitchers are famous for being bad hitters. Because of that, they are often called on to bunt when they have to hit. In 2016, Cubs pitcher Jon Lester was pressed into duty as a pinch hitter in an extra-inning game against the visiting Seattle Mariners.

With Jason Heyward on third and one out, Lester stepped in. When the count reached two strikes, the defense relaxed. Players don't usually bunt with two strikes, because a foul ball is a strikeout. With the game on the line, Cubs manager Joe Maddon called for the suicide squeeze. As Mariners reliever Cody Martin began his windup, Heyward took off from third. Lester laid down a perfect bunt. Martin raced in and scooped the ball to the catcher, but Heyward beat the tag. His teammates mobbed Lester, tearing off his jersey in celebration of the 6–5 walk-off win.

PIRATE POWER

In a 162-game season, an occasional walk-off play can energize a team. The 1959 Pirates delivered 18 in a single season. Pirates star Bill Mazeroski led the team with four walk-off game winners. The team even hit walk-offs in both games of a doubleheader! Pitcher Roy Face set a Major League record by winning his first 17 starts of the season. Nine of those wins came thanks to walk-off hits.

Jon Lester drops down his game-winning bunt.

INSIDE-THE-PARK WALK-OFF

In San Francisco, a large section of the right field wall is built to look like an old-school brick warehouse. Balls that hit this unusual wall carry a long way if the outfielder doesn't grab them immediately.

The Giants trailed the visiting Colorado Rockies 5–4 in the bottom of the 10th inning. With a runner at second, Giants outfielder Ángel Pagán fell behind 0–1 in the count. He crushed a ball to right field that

KINGS OF THE WALK-OFF

Only five players in Major League history have delivered more than 20 walk-off hits. All but Dusty Baker are in the Baseball Hall of Fame.

1 Frank Robinson, 26
2 Tony Perez, 22
3 Dusty Baker, 21
4 Andre Dawson, 20
5 Roberto Clemente, 20

hit the bottom of the wall. The ball came off the wall hard, shooting past Rockies outfielder Michael Cuddyer. Pagán hustled from the crack of the bat. He had a chance to win the game with an inside-the-park home run. Pagan slid headfirst around the tag of catcher Wilin Rosario. He swiped the plate just ahead of the tag for the win.

Ángel Pagán chugs toward home with the game on the line.

PAPI POWER

The New York Yankees faced the Boston Red Sox in the 2004 American League Championship Series.

Game 4 was tied 4–4 in the bottom of the 12th inning. Manny Ramirez led off with a single for the Red Sox. Designated hitter David "Big Papi" Ortiz had a chance to win the game with one swing of the bat. His 41 home runs in the regular season were second in the American League to Ramirez' 43.

With the count 2–1, Yankees reliever Paul Quantrill threw Ortiz a fastball. Big Papi hit a game-winning walk-off home run into the bullpen in right field. The Red Sox were still alive.

The next night Ortiz came to the plate in extra innings with the game tied 4–4. This time it was the 14th inning and there were two runners on base. Ortiz delivered once again. He capped a 10-pitch at-bat with a bloop hit to center field. It brought Johnny Damon home from second and gave the Sox back-to-back walk-off wins.

David Ortiz watches his drive in the 12th inning of Game 4 in a playoff series against the Yankees.

David Ortiz played in 85 postseason games in nine seasons and had three walk-off hits. All three came in the 2004 postseason when he led the Red Sox to the World Series title.

CHAPTER FOUR

PITCHING PERFECTION

KING OF STRIKEOUTS

Most walk-offs happen because the winning team's pitcher kept them in the game. In Game 2 of the 2017 American League Championship Series, Houston ace Justin Verlander did just that.

With Houston leading the series 1–0, he shut down the powerful Yankees lineup. Verlander struck out 13 Yankees and held them to one run in nine innings.

Justin Verlander delivers a pitch against the Yankees.

With the score tied at 1–1, the Astros had a chance to finish off Verlander's complete game. After José Altuve singled to left, shortstop

STRIKEOUT ENDINGS

The best defense is to not let a batter hit the ball.
These ten modern-day pitchers clinched the World
Series with walk-off strikeouts.

	PITCHER	YEAR	BATTER
1	Daniel Hudson	2019	Michael Brantley
2	Chris Sale	2018	Manny Machado
3	Wade Davis	2015	Wilmer Flores
4	Koji Uehara	2013	Matt Carpenter
5	Sergio Romo	2012	Miguel Cabrera
6	Brian Wilson	2010	Nelson Cruz
7	Brad Lidge	2008	Eric Hinske
8	Jonathan Papelbon	2007	Seth Smith
9	Adam Wainwright	2006	Brandon Inge
10	Orel Hershiser	1988	Tony Phillips

Carlos Correa came to the plate. With the count
3–2, Correa got a pitch he liked. He drove a ball to
the opposite field. As Altuve rounded second, he
got the go sign from third base coach Gary Pettis.
The Yankees executed the relay in time to throw the
speedy Altuve out. Unfortunately, Yankee catcher
Gary Sánchez bobbled the throw as Altuve slid past
him for the walk-off win.

ENDING THE DROUGHT

Chicago Cubs pitcher Mike Montgomery entered Game 7 of the 2016 World Series with two outs in the 10th inning. His team led the Cleveland Indians 8–7. Cleveland had a runner at first, and the winning run at home plate. Montgomery had to get one out to bring Chicago its first World Series in 108 years. With the world watching, Montgomery had the chance to end the longest title drought in professional sports. One bad pitch, and it would be the Indians celebrating.

Michael Martínez was at the plate for Cleveland. He swung at the 0–1 pitch from Montgomery. The ball was a slow chopper to third. Cubs infielder Kris Bryant raced in and scooped up the ball. He fired a strike to first base for the final out. For the first time in more than 100 years, the Cubs were World Champions!

Mike Montgomery delivers a pitch in Game 7 of the 2016 World Series.

The 1908 Cubs won the World Series for the third year in a row. Few people would have guessed the team wouldn't get another championship for more than 100 years. The 1908 team included four players who are in baseball's Hall of Fame.

PITCHING PERFECTION

Only 23 pitchers in history have tossed a perfect game. It is considered the most difficult feat for a pitcher. Only one man has ever thrown a perfect game in the World Series.

Don Larsen took the mound for the New York Yankees on October 8, 1956. It was Game 5, and the series was tied 2–2. Larsen was not a dominant pitcher. He finished his big league career with an 81–91 record. But for one day in 1956, he was the best pitcher in baseball.

Larsen had faced 26 batters and sat down every one of them. No walks, no errors, no fielder's choices, and no hit batsmen. Pinch hitter Dale Mitchell came to the plate. He was the Brooklyn Dodgers' 27th batter and last hope. He was no match for Larsen, who struck him out looking. Larsen's walk-off moment is a record that has never been repeated.

In the eighth inning, a Yankee Stadium scoreboard showed Larsen's progress toward a perfect game.

TEXAS HEAT

Hall of Famer Nolan Ryan pitched for 27 seasons and only gave up one walk-off home run in his career. Rather, Ryan was known for doing the walking off. His Major League record seven no-hitters were the ultimate walk-offs for a pitcher.

At 44 years old, Ryan was still going strong for the Texas Rangers. He faced the Toronto Blue Jays at home on May 1, 1991. Ryan was dominant. He struck out 15 batters through the first eight innings. The Rangers led 3–0, and Ryan found himself one out away from his seventh career no-hitter.

Standing in his way was future Hall of Famer Roberto Alomar. Ryan ran the count to two balls and two strikes. The home crowd was on their feet cheering Ryan on. He blew a fastball past Alomar and walked off the mound with his seventh no-hitter.

Nolan Ryan's teammates lifted him onto their shoulders after a 1990 no-hitter. It was the sixth no-hitter of his long career.

Roberto Alomar was the walk-off out in Ryan's seventh no-hitter. His dad, Sandy Alomar, was the first out in Ryan's first no-hitter in 1973.

CHAPTER FIVE

WORLD SERIES WINNERS

BREGMAN BOMB

The 2017 World Series was a battle of 100-win teams. The Los Angeles Dodgers led the Major League with 104 wins during the regular season. The Houston Astros topped the American League with 101 wins. The two pennant winners battled for seven games in the 2017 World Series.

With the series tied 2–2, the teams faced off in Houston for Game 5. Each team exploded for 12 runs, setting up a dramatic finish.

The Astros had runners on first and second with two outs in the bottom of the 10th. Astros third baseman Alex Bregman stepped in against Dodgers reliever Kenley Jansen. Bregman jumped on the first pitch, lining it to left field. Dodgers outfielder Andre Ethier came up throwing. He delivered a strike to the plate. But rookie Derek Fisher beat the throw. The Astros took Game 5 by a score of 13–12 and went on to win the 2017 World Series.

There have been 16 walk-off home runs in World Series games. The Yankees top the list with four of those 16 homers.

EVERY WORLD SERIES WINNING WALK-OFF IN HISTORY

These players delivered walk-off hits to seal a World Series championship for their team.

YEAR	TYPE	PLAYER	TEAM
1924	Single to left	Earl McNeely	Senators
1927	Wild pitch	Earle Combs (scored)	Yankees
1929	Double	Bing Miller	Athletics
1935	Single to right	Goose Goslin	Tigers
1953	Single to center	Billy Martin	Yankees
1960	Solo home run	Bill Mazeroski	Pirates
1991	Single to left	Gene Larkin	Twins
1993	Three-run homer	Joe Carter	Blue Jays
1997	Single to center	Edgar Renteria	Marlins
2001	Single to center	Luis Gonzalez	Rockies

MAX-IMUM LONG BALL

After their heartbreaking loss in 2017, the Dodgers made it back to the World Series in 2018. They faced off against the Boston Red Sox. Trailing 2–0 in the series, the Dodgers needed a win in Game 3.

The game was tied 1–1 after nine innings. In the 15th inning, Max Muncy stepped to the plate for the Dodgers. He crushed what looked like a walk-off home run to right. But the ball hooked foul at the last second.

WHO SAID THAT?

Today the term *walk-off* makes fans think of a wild, game-winning celebration. The term began as a negative comment. Hall of Fame pitcher Dennis Eckersley first used the term in the 1980s. He originally called it a "walk-off piece." Eckersley said that was when a pitcher gave up the game-winner and had to walk off the mound in defeat.

Muncy got another shot in the bottom of the 18th. Red Sox reliever Nathan Eovaldi delivered a pitch that Muncy hit high and deep to left center field. Muncy raised his arms in celebration as the ball landed in the bleachers for the walk-off winner. Unfortunately for Dodgers fans, it was the only game Los Angeles would win in the series. The Red Sox took the title 4–1.

Max Muncy celebrates his 18th-inning blast.

LIMPING INTO HISTORY

In 1988, Dennis Eckersley was the best closer in baseball. The Oakland Athletics star led MLB with 45 saves. He had just earned the American League Championship Series MVP award. He looked unstoppable.

In Game 1 of the World Series, the A's held a 4–3 lead in the bottom of the ninth. Eckersley was called in to get three outs. With two outs and a runner at first, Dodgers manager Tommy Lasorda called on his star player Kirk Gibson to pinch hit. Gibson was out with two bad legs. As he limped to the plate, the home crowd went wild!

Gibson worked the count to 3–2. Then, on the eighth pitch, he struck. He sent Eckersley's backdoor slider 370 feet to right field and over the fence. As he reached home plate, his teammates surrounded him to celebrate an epic walk-off win!

The walk-off homer Kirk Gibson hit off of Dennis Eckersley in Game 1 was his only at-bat of the entire 1988 World Series.

Kirk Gibson's swing was slightly awkward, but he managed to hit the ball deep.

DAZZLING BY THE DECADE

There have been so many amazing walk-offs in Major League history. It would be impossible to pick the best of all time. So how about the best from each decade? Here are some memorable walk-offs from each decade of the last 100 years.

▶ 1920s: Muddy Ruel scored the walk-off winning run in the bottom of the 12th inning to give the Washington Senators the 1924 World Series. Ruel scored on a base hit by teammate Earl McNeely.

▶ 1930s: Yankees Hall of Famer Joe Sewell only hit one walk-off home run in his big league career. It came in the bottom of the 11th inning of a 1931 game against the Detroit Tigers. The three-run blast gave the home team the win.

▶ 1940s: Ted Williams is considered by many to be the greatest pure hitter of all time. Though it didn't count in the standings, his walk-off three-run home run to win the 1941 All-Star Game is a great moment in baseball history.

▶ 1950s: Giants bench player Dusty Rhodes won Game 1 of the 1954 World Series with a pinch-hit, three-run home run. The Giants went on to sweep the Cleveland Indians in four games.

▶ 1960s: Yankee legend Mickey Mantle won Game 3 of the 1964 World Series with a walk-off home run on the first pitch he saw in the bottom of the ninth. Legend has it that Mantle called his shot before he got to the plate.

► 1970s: Red Sox catcher Carlton Fisk's walk-off home run in the bottom of the 12th inning to win Game 6 of the 1975 World Series is legendary, even though the Reds won the title in Game 7. Fisk's waving the ball back into fair territory and the fans charging onto the field added to the drama.

► 1980s: Mookie Wilson drove in Ray Knight to walk off Game 6 of the 1986 World Series. Wilson hit a slow roller to first that should have ended the inning. But the ball went through Red Sox first baseman Bill Buckner's legs.

► 1990s: World Series winning walk-offs are rare. There have only been 11 in history. Marlins shortstop Edgar Renteria's line drive walk-off single to win the 1997 World Series tops the 1990s.

► 2000s: Oakland A's pinch hitter Scott Hatteberg crushed a home run to left field against the Kansas City Royals in 2002. The walk-off was huge because it gave the A's their 20th win in a row, an American League all-time record.

► 2010s: Edwin Encarnación ended the 2016 American League Wild Card game with one swing. The Blue Jays slugger crushed a walk-off homer off of Baltimore reliever Ubaldo Jiménez to advance Toronto to the divisional round of the playoffs.

GLOSSARY

closer (KLOHZ-er)—pitcher brought in during the late innings, usually to save the game

legendary (LEJ-uhnd-air-ee)—something or someone that is well-known or famous

pennant (PEN-uhnt)—a triangular flag that symbolizes a league championship

perfect game (PUR-fikt GAME)—a game in which a pitcher doesn't allow a single batter to reach first base

save (SAYV)—when a relief pitcher protects a team's lead at the end of the game

strategy (STRAT-uh-jee)—a careful plan or method

suicide squeeze (SOO-uh-side SKWEEZ)—a play in which the runner on third base runs all out for home plate as the pitcher throws the ball; the runner does so without knowing whether the batter will contact the ball

walk-off (WALK-off)—a game-winning hit in the bottom half of the last inning

READ MORE

Chandler, Matt. *Pro Baseball Records: A Guide for Every Fan.* North Mankato, MN: Capstone Press, 2019.

Richards, Jon. *Baseball Superstars 2019.* New York: Carlton Books, 2019.

Velasco, Catherine Ann. *Behind the Scenes of Pro Baseball.* North Mankato, MN: Capstone Press, 2019.

INTERNET SITES

National Baseball Hall of Fame
www.baseballhall.org

Negro Leagues Baseball Museum
www.nlbm.com

Official Site of Major League Baseball
www.mlb.com

INDEX